RED PANDAS

by *Josh Gregory*

Children's Press®

An Imprint of Scholastic Inc.

Content Consultant
Dr. Stephen S. Ditchkoff
Professor of Wildlife Ecology and Management
Auburn University
Auburn, Alabama

Photographs ©: cover: Toshiaki Ida/Nature Production/Minden
Pictures; 1: Isselee/Dreamstime; 2-3 background: Thisisdon/
Dreamstime; 2 foreground: Chris Godfrey Wildlife Photography/Alamy
Images; 4, 5 background: Angelo Cavalli/Getty Images; 5 top: Patrick
Rolands/Dreamstime; 5 bottom: FEATURECHINA/Zhu Minsong/
Newscom; 7: Kotomiti_okuma/Dreamstime; 8: CSP_michaklootwijk/
age fotostock; 11: DINODIA/age fotostock; 12: Patrick Rolands/
Dreamstime; 15: Chris Humphries/Shutterstock, Inc.; 16: Chris Godfrey
Wildlife Photography/Alamy Images; 19: McPHOTO/Blickwinkel/
age fotostock; 20: Dave Henrys/Alamy Images; 23: Angelo Cavalli/
Getty Images; 24: Jimmy Jeong/The Canadian Press/AP Images; 27:
WILDLIFE GmbH/Alamy Images; 28: The Natural History Museum/
Alamy Images; 31: Hero Images/Getty Images; 32: John Shaw/
Science Source; 35: Top Photo Corporation/Alamy Images; 36:
Danita Delimont/Alamy Images; 39: robert salthouse/Alamy Images;
40: FEATURECHINA/Zhu Minsong/Newscom; 44-45 background:
Thisisdon/Dreamstime; 46: Isselee/Dreamstime.

Maps by Bob Italiano.

Library of Congress Cataloging-in-Publication Data
Names: Gregory, Josh, author.
Title: Red pandas / by Josh Gregory.
Other titles: Nature's children (New York, N.Y.)
Description: New York : Children's Press, an imprint of Scholastic Inc.,
   [2017] | Series: Nature's children | Includes bibliographical
   references and index.
Identifiers: LCCN 2015043584| ISBN 9780531230305
(library binding : alk. paper) | ISBN 9780531219362 (pbk. : alk. paper)
Subjects: LCSH: Red panda—Juvenile literature.
Classification: LCC QL737.C214 G7425 2017 | DDC 599.76/3—dc23
LC record available at http://lccn.loc.gov/2015043584

Printed in China 62
SCHOLASTIC, CHILDREN'S PRESS, and associated logos are trademarks
and/or registered trademarks of Scholastic Inc.

1 2 3 4 5 6 7 8 9 10 R 26 25 24 23 22 21 20 19 18 17

Red Pandas

Class	Mammalia
Order	Carnivora
Family	Ailuridae
Genus	*Ailurus*
Species	*Ailurus fulgens*
World distribution	China, Nepal, Bhutan, Myanmar, India
Habitat	Forests
Distinctive physical characteristics	Covered in thick, soft fur; most of the body is a reddish color; underside is black; face is white and brown; soles of the feet are covered in white fur; roughly the size of a domestic cat; long, furry, red tail ringed in brown; claws are semi-retractable; extended wrist bone functions as a sort of thumb
Habits	Generally nocturnal; most active at dawn and dusk; usually solitary, except during mating season; spends most of its time in treetops; has strong climbing abilities; communicates using scent, sound, and body language
Diet	Primarily bamboo; also eats other plants, as well as eggs, insects, and small birds

Contents

CHAPTER 1

Red Streak

In the forests along the slopes of the Himalaya Mountains, dense plant growth makes it difficult to see very far in any direction. The branches of tall trees form a ceiling of leaves overhead. Stalks of bamboo sprout from the ground below. The sounds of insects, birds, and other animals fill the air.

If you look up, you might spot a flash of red fur dashing across the branches. If you're especially lucky, the animal might pause long enough for you to get a good look at it. Is it some sort of raccoon? A cat? No, neither of those guesses is quite right. It's a red panda! This rare and beautiful animal is getting ready to spend the evening **foraging** for something to eat. After looking around to make sure there are no dangers below, the panda dashes down the trunk of a tree. Then it quickly disappears into a cluster of bamboo.

Red pandas are very good at darting through the treetops.

Small, Soft, and Furry

Red pandas are named for the thick, red fur that covers most of their body. They are not completely red from nose to tail, though. A red panda's underside is a deep shade of black. Its face is mostly white, with brown markings around and below its eyes. Its ears and the bottoms of its paws are also white. Its tail is mostly red, but it also has rings of a brownish color.

The average red panda is about the size of a typical house cat. From its nose to the base of its tail, it might measure roughly 20 to 26 inches (51 to 66 centimeters). The tail is quite long. It measures an additional 12 to 20 inches (30.5 to 51 cm). The animal can weigh anywhere from 6.5 to 14 pounds (3 to 6 kilograms).

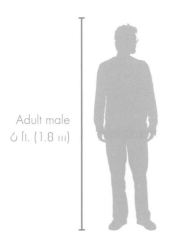

Adult male
6 ft. (1.8 m)

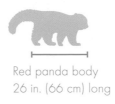

Red panda body
26 in. (66 cm) long

A red panda dozes in a tree.

Mountain Homes

Red pandas are most often found in the forests of the Himalayas. They also live in other forest **habitats** located nearby. The Himalayas form a huge mountain range. It spans a large part of Asia. Red pandas do not live throughout the entire mountain range. They make their homes specifically in the countries of Nepal, Myanmar, Bhutan, India, and China.

There are a few different elements that together form the perfect home for a red panda. Red pandas live mostly in habitats where plenty of bamboo grows. This plant is an important food source for pandas. There are also a lot of tall trees in the areas where red pandas like to be. Trees provide places for the pandas to live and sleep. Finally, red pandas prefer to make their homes where there are many logs, tree stumps, and plants covering the forest floor. Such dense covering helps the animals stay out of sight as they move around on the ground.

Red pandas spend a lot of time in trees, where it is easy for them to stay hidden.

CHAPTER 2

Surviving in the Himalayas

On most days, a red panda's main goal is simply to find and eat plenty of food. The animal might eat up to 45 percent of its own weight in food each day. The amount of foraging needed to gather this much food can take up to half of the red panda's waking hours. Bamboo makes up the bulk of its diet. Red pandas especially like to eat the plant's leaves and shoots. Red pandas also eat parts of many other plants. Fruit, acorns, flowers, and roots are all part of a red panda's diet. Sometimes, red pandas capture prey such as insects, small birds, and rodents.

A red panda uses its front paws to grab and bring food to its mouth to eat. Its strong jaws and teeth are perfect for chewing up tough plant materials. A red panda can also drink using its paw. It dips the paw in water and then drinks from it like a cup.

A red panda takes a bite out of some leaves.

Sniff Sniff

Red pandas do not have especially powerful senses. Unlike many animals, they aren't able to spot food from great distances or hear threats approaching from miles away. Nevertheless, their ability to observe the world around them helps them socialize and stay alive.

Smell is a red panda's most important sense. Catching the scent of an approaching **predator** can give a red panda time to escape.

Red pandas also create their own unique scents. They have special **glands** that produce these distinctive odors. Red pandas rub against trees and other surfaces to spread these scents throughout their home areas. This lets red pandas know when they have entered another red panda's home **territory**. Scent is also used to attract **mates**, and red panda mothers even rely on scents to recognize their own babies.

A red panda's sense of smell helps it find food.

Run, Jump, and Climb

Red pandas often spend time on the ground when they are foraging. But they live most of their lives in the treetops. Because they are very good at running and climbing, they have no trouble going back and forth between the forest floor and the trees. They use their sharp claws to grip the sides of trees as they climb. The thick fur on the bottoms of their paws makes their hold even stronger. This is especially helpful in snowy or icy conditions.

Each of a red panda's front paws has a special wrist bone that sticks out a bit. Red pandas can use these bones like thumbs. They help the pandas grasp branches as they climb and run through the treetops. A red panda's long tail also comes in handy when the animal runs across narrow branches. The panda uses its tail to stay balanced and keep from falling to the ground.

FUN FACT! Red pandas always climb down trees headfirst.

Strong claws help a red panda grip a tree trunk or branch.

Staying Safe

Red pandas must keep a close lookout for predators. Their biggest threat comes from snow leopards, which are very fast and can climb trees. Dholes are another common predator. These wild dogs might look like pets, but they are deadly hunters.

Red pandas have a feature that helps them to avoid predators. Their fur helps them stay hidden when they climb in trees. It has the same colors as some of the moss and **lichen** that grow on the trees, so it blends right in. When moving along the ground, red pandas try to stay out of sight among the dense plant cover.

Sometimes a red panda can't avoid being spotted. If it is not able to run away, it might try to fight off a predator. When threatened, a red panda often rears back on its hind legs. It then lashes out with its sharp front claws. It may also release an unpleasant scent from its glands. This smell can be bad enough to drive predators away.

Red pandas need to be especially alert for possible dangers when they are on the ground.

CHAPTER 3

Rivals, Mates, and Babies

Red pandas are **nocturnal**. They spend most daylight hours sleeping. Being asleep while the sun is up helps red pandas beat the heat when the weather is warm. It also helps them stay out of sight of predators.

Every evening, a red panda wakes from its resting place up in the branches of a tree. Before doing anything else, it might take time to **groom** itself. Red pandas stay clean by licking their paws and then rubbing their paws all over their fur. This helps clear away dirt, twigs, and any other materials that might have clung to the red panda's fur.

Once it is clean, the red panda might move through its territory to leave scent markings. These markings don't last forever. As a result, the panda must reapply them regularly to keep rivals away. After marking its territory, the red panda has probably worked up an appetite. It sets off for a night of foraging.

A red panda grooms itself carefully.

Face-to-Face

Adult red pandas are mostly solitary. In rare cases, however, they might socialize or travel in pairs or small family groups. They also spend time together during mating season.

While scents are the main way red pandas communicate, they also use a variety of sounds to express themselves. Baby red pandas make high-pitched whistling noises when they are scared. Adults bark loudly when they face danger. They can also make snorts, squeals, sighs, and other sounds.

Body language is another important communication tool for red pandas. For example, when two rival red pandas face off, they stare each other in the eyes and arch their backs. They then begin quickly bobbing their heads up and down. They do this to intimidate each other. One of the red pandas might be scared away by the other's display.

FUN FACT! The red panda is the official state animal of Sikkim, a state in India.

Red pandas rarely spend time around one another.

Mating Season

From about January to April, it is mating reason for red pandas. During this time, red pandas become much more social than usual. They gather in groups, and they might play by wrestling or biting one another. At the same time, males use their scents to advertise that they are looking for mates. If a female is ready, she chooses a mate based on these scents. Each female is able to become pregnant for only a couple of days out of the year. However, both males and females might mate with many different partners during the mating season.

A red panda is ready to give birth about 130 days after mating. A few days before giving birth, she builds a nest for the babies. She first finds a secure, hidden spot. Then she carries sticks, leaves, and other materials to it and uses them to create the nest.

FUN FACT! Red pandas usually live for about 8 to 10 years in the wild.

A newborn red panda is unable to feed or protect itself.

From Birth to Adulthood

A red panda litter typically contains just one or two babies. Up to four can be born at a time, though this is rare. Red panda babies are born with their eyes and ears closed. They do not have red fur at first. Instead, they are fluffy and gray. Because the newborn babies are helpless, they stay in the nest where it is safe. Their food is milk that they drink from their mother.

Baby red pandas open their eyes and ears after about two or three weeks. Their fur starts changing to look more like an adult's. At about six to seven weeks, the babies start moving around the nest. They play with each other and groom each other. Their mother begins bringing them bamboo to chew on. When they are about three months old, the babies start leaving the nest. They stay close to their mother as they learn to forage and avoid danger. When the next mating season begins, their mother chases them away so she can prepare to have more babies.

A red panda mother holds on to her baby while moving through a tree.

CHAPTER 4

A Unique Animal

Red pandas have been on Earth for millions of years. Long ago, they lived in places nowhere near their current homes. For example, red panda **fossils** have been discovered as far away as North America. Over time, the red panda's **range** shrank to what it is today.

People who are native to the red panda's home countries have known about the animal for a very long time. Scientists from outside these places first recorded the animal's existence in the 1820s. French **zoologist** Frédéric Cuvier named it. He called the animal *Ailurus fulgens*. This name comes from the ancient Greek words for "cat" and "fire."

Today, the red panda is sometimes divided into two **subspecies.** They are called the western red panda and the Styan's red panda. The Styan's red panda is larger than the western subspecies. Also, its fur is a brighter shade of red.

Images of red pandas first reached Europe in the 19th century.

Classification Controversy

Scientists work hard to organize species into categories based on a number of factors. These elements include animals' physical features and whether they have **ancestors** in common. Sometimes this can be a long and complicated process.

At first, red pandas were grouped with an animal called the giant panda. However, scientists eventually realized that the two species were not as closely related as they had thought. Experts later placed red pandas in a family alongside raccoons and other similar animals. Red pandas share many traits with raccoons. However, scientists later learned that they were not actually close relatives. They were able to figure this out because modern technology enabled them to study the animals' DNA. This provided much more accurate information about how the red panda was related to other animals. Scientists soon determined that red pandas actually belonged in a family that is separate from all other animals.

Scientists studying DNA can learn a huge amount of information about living things.

Another Kind of Panda

Scientists no longer group the red panda and giant panda together in the same family. However, these animals still have a lot more in common than just a name. For example, while they are not extremely close relatives, they do probably share a common ancestor. The two animals share a similar diet as well. They both consume large amounts of bamboo every day, occasionally eating small animals, too. Giant pandas even have the same sort of wrist bones that red pandas have. This allows them to grip bamboo stalks and climb trees.

Like the red panda, the giant panda lives in mountain habitats. The range it occupies, however, is much smaller than that of the red panda. The giant panda is one of the world's rarest animals. It is found only in parts of China. There are about 1,800 of them living in the wild today, making them highly **endangered**.

Red pandas and giant pandas both have a diet that consists largely of bamboo.

CHAPTER 5

Pandas and People

Red pandas tend to live in remote areas where most people do not travel. Nevertheless, they have many interactions with humans. One reason for this is the red panda's appealing looks. Its beautiful red fur, small size, and cute face make it the kind of animal people are eager to see up close. Red pandas are also playful and fun to watch in action. They can even be tamed somewhat and taught to perform tricks. This makes people want to keep them as pets or see them at zoos.

Unfortunately, humans have largely had a negative impact on the red panda. Today, this remarkable animal is in danger of disappearing. Fewer than 3,000 adult red pandas remain in wild habitats. Even worse, that number is declining.

Zoos offer people the chance to see red pandas up close.

Hunted

One reason for the red panda's declining population is illegal hunting. The very characteristics that make red pandas so fascinating also encourage people to trap and even kill them. Sometimes hunters trap the animals and then sell them as pets. Other times, **poachers** kill them to sell their furs. The furs are made into hats and other clothing. While it is illegal to hunt red pandas, poachers do it anyway. They can make a great deal of money selling these rare animals.

Red pandas also face danger from hunters who do not target them. In many of the areas where red pandas live, hunters use traps to catch deer, wild pigs, and other kinds of animals for their meat. However, red pandas can get caught in these traps just as easily as other animals do.

Hats made with red panda fur are traditional in parts of the Himalayan region.

Fewer Trees, Fewer Pandas

Hunting isn't the only thing causing the red panda population to decrease. Another major problem is that their homes are disappearing at an alarming rate. As the human population increases, people clear away more of the planet's forests. Sometimes they do this to gather wood. Other times, they do it to make room for farms, houses, roads, and other construction projects. Either way, these actions leave less space where red pandas can live. They also leave groups of red pandas cut off from other members of their species. This can make it much harder for red pandas to find mates and reproduce.

As people establish homes and farms closer to red panda habitats, other problems also occur. For example, livestock on farms might compete with red pandas for food. Pet dogs may attack them. These other animals can even spread deadly diseases to the pandas.

Logging removes the trees red pandas rely on to survive.

Protecting Pandas

Conservation groups are hard at work trying to prevent the situation from becoming any worse for red pandas. One of their activities is working with people who live in areas where red pandas are common. They share information about how to protect red pandas and why it is important. They also teach people ways to avoid harming the animals while hunting or gathering resources from the forest. Some groups hire local people to observe red panda populations and to look out for potential problems.

Another strategy involves captive breeding. This is when red pandas are captured from the wild and brought to a location such as a zoo. There, the pandas can reproduce in safety. Once the babies are old enough, they are released into the wild.

With the help of such programs, red pandas might have a chance at survival. However, they still face many obstacles. Only one thing is certain: We should do everything we can to make sure these amazing animals remain a part of our planet.

A researcher cares for a baby red panda at a research center in China.

Words to Know

ancestors (AN-ses-turz) — ancient animal species that are related to modern species

conservation (kahn-sur-VAY-shuhn) — the protection of valuable things, especially forests, wildlife, natural resources, or artistic or historic objects

DNA (DEE-EN-AY) — the molecule that carries our genes, found inside the nucleus of cells; DNA is short for deoxyribonucleic acid

endangered (en-DAYN-jurd) — at risk of becoming extinct, usually because of human activity

foraging (FOR-ij-ing) — going in search of food

fossils (FAH-suhlz) — the hardened remains of prehistoric plants and animals

glands (GLANDZ) — organs in the body that produce or release natural chemicals

groom (GROOM) — to brush and clean

habitats (HAB-uh-tats) — places where an animal or a plant is usually found

lichen (LYE-kuhn) — a flat, spongelike growth on rocks, walls, and trees that consists of algae and fungi growing close together

mates (MAYTS) — animals that join together to produce babies

nocturnal (nahk-TUR-nuhl) — active at night

poachers (POH-churz) — people who hunt or fish illegally

predator (PREH-duh-tur) — an animal that lives by hunting other animals for food

prey (PRAY) — an animal that is hunted by another animal for food

range (RAYNJ) — an area of land in which an animal confines its daily activities

shoots (SHOOTS) — new sprouts or twigs growing from the main trunk or stem of a plant or tree

subspecies (SUB-spee-sheez) — groups of animals that are part of the same species but share important differences

territory (TER-uh-tor-ee) — an area of land claimed by a given individual or group

zoologist (zoh-AH-luh-jist) — a person who studies animal life

Habitat Map

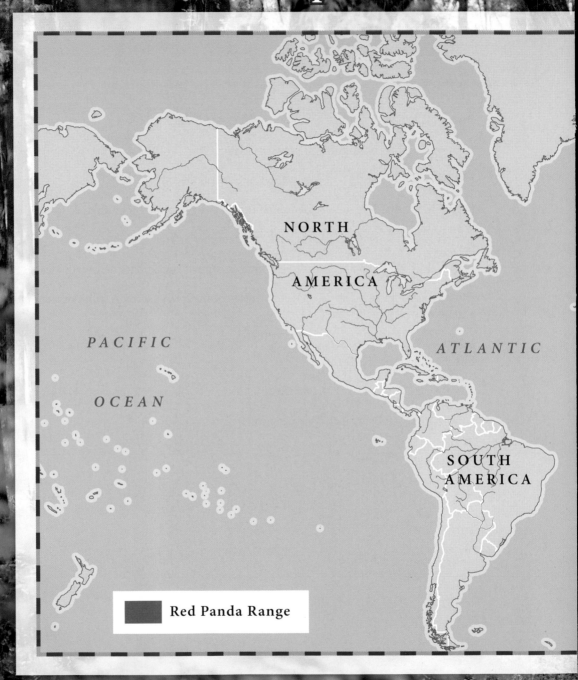

NORTH AMERICA

SOUTH AMERICA

PACIFIC OCEAN

ATLANTIC

Red Panda Range

ARCTIC OCEAN

EUROPE

ASIA

AFRICA

PACIFIC OCEAN

OCEAN

INDIAN

OCEAN

AUSTRALIA

Find Out More

Book

Antill, Sara. *Red Panda*. New York: Windmill Books, 2011.

Visit this Scholastic Web site for more information on red pandas:
www.factsfornow.scholastic.com
Enter the keywords **Red Pandas**

Index

Page numbers in *italics* indicate a photograph or map.

About the Author

Josh Gregory is the author of more than 90 books for kids. He has written about everything from animals to technology to history. A graduate of the University of Missouri-Columbia, he currently lives in Portland, Oregon.